CHOSEN

Bishop Lorenzo N. Peterson

Co-Authors

Saquoye J. Tarver
Dr. Juanita Woodson

Copyright © 2019 by Bishop Lorenzo Peterson

All rights reserved. This book or any portion thereof may not be reproduced or used in any manner whatsoever without the express written permission of the publisher except for the use of brief quotations in a book review.

Scriptures marked KJV are taken from the KING JAMES VERSION (KJV): KING JAMES VERSION, public domain.

Scriptures marked ESV are taken from the THE HOLY BIBLE, ENGLISH STANDARD VERSION (ESV): Scriptures taken from THE HOLY BIBLE, ENGLISH STANDARD VERSION ® Copyright© 2001 by Crossway, a publishing ministry of Good News Publishers. Used by permission.

Scriptures marked AMP are taken from the AMPLIFIED BIBLE (AMP): Scripture taken from the AMPLIFIED® BIBLE, Copyright © 1954, 1958, 1962, 1964, 1965, 1987 by the Lockman Foundation Used by Permission. (www.Lockman.org)

ISBN - 978-1-7330800-2-6
Printed in the United States of America
First Printing, 2019
Impact Development Foundation Inc.
Impact Book Publishing Co

950 Eagles Landing Pkwy
Suite #722
Stockbridge GA, 30281
www.impactbookco.com

In the Gospel of John 15:16 KJV, it is written in the English language, "Ye have not chosen me, but I have chosen you, and ordained you, that ye should go and bring forth fruit, and that your fruit should remain: that whatsoever ye shall ask of the Father in my name, he may give it to you". Throughout the ages God has chosen and handpicked those whom He desired to carry out special tasks for Kingdom purposes. Many times, those being selected may have felt unprepared and not worthy, incapable, and some may have felt out of place. Nonetheless, you were **chosen**… not by men but by God. Therefore, you have everything you need through God in order to complete your God given task. Please remember, that you are never alone, "lo, He will be with you always, even unto the end of the world Amen." (Matthew 28:20 b KJV).

Table of Contents

* * * * *

CHAPTER 1: FOLLOWING THE ANOINTING 1

CHAPTER 2: SELF EXAMINATION 21

CHAPTER 3: GOD'S REQUIRED ACTION PLAN FOR SPIRITUAL LEADERSHIP 35

CHAPTER 4: SEVENFOLD PURPOSE OF THE PASTOR. .47

CHAPTER 5: TEAMWORK MAKES THE DREAM WORK 57

CHAPTER 6: TOGETHER WE CAN .67

CHAPTER 7: A LEGACY OF INFLUENCE: LEAVING YOUR MARK. 79

ABOUT THE AUTHOR 91

Chapter 1
FOLLOWING THE ANOINTING

"Following the Anointing"

Following the anointing should be paramount in the life of a leader and believer alike. The anointing is what truly makes the difference. In fact, being effective to the capacity that God has called you to is ultimately impossible without it. It is possible to do the work of the Lord successfully to a certain degree depending solely on your own strength, intellect, etc... However, those things will never yield the benefits of depending on the anointing of God above everything else.

One benefit of following the anointing is that favor is released in your life. David is a great example of the favor of God being released in his life due to him following the anointing. 1 Chronicles 14:1 says: "Now Hiram king of Tyre sent messengers to David, and timber of cedars, with masons and carpenters, to build him a house." The favor of God brings about necessary resources. When you follow the anointing you have confidence that God will provide you with what you need to accomplish His work.

As you move forward in the work of the Lord walk in humility with an understanding that it is not exclusively about you. In fact, your elevation is personable, not personal. God has mandated you to meet the needs of the people he has called you to.

We see in 1 Chronicles 14:2, "David perceived that the LORD had confirmed him king over Israel, for his kingdom was lifted up on high, because of his people Israel. God had the people in mind more so than David.

Striving to have a good reputation should be the personal effort of a leader. In order to accomplish this and shield yourself from a tarnished reputation you must resist and subdue sensual desires. Casual sin will tarnish your reputation.

David fell subject to sensual desires by taking more wives and concubines after the Lord had instructed him not to do so. God told him not to be multiplied in wives because they would lead his heart away from Him. (Deuteronomy 17:16-18)

Following the instructions of the Lord while leading God's people protects you from falling into sin. It is possible to be a leader of integrity when you follow what God instructs much rather than the desires of your flesh. Walking upright before the Lord is only possible with the help of Holy Spirit. He will empower you to walk in the Spirit so that you will not gratify the desires of the flesh. (Galatians 5:16) This will ensure that you remain a positive example before those you lead concerning what it looks like to live a life surrendered to God.

Although you may strive and position yourself to be an honorable leader in the sight of the Lord and people, it's important to note that elevations and promotions are normally accompanied with new battles. As much as an oxymoron this may seem, being anointed to do the work of the Lord, often comes with public attacks from the enemy. Expect the enemy to make a grand show of force to test you. 1 Chronicles 14:9 is a great illustration of this kind of attack. The scripture states "they spread themselves in the valley Rephaim, with their gods present." All of this took place when the Philistines heard that David was anointed king over all Israel, all the Philistines went up to see David.

The beautiful thing was that David wasn't afraid because he was confident that God was with him. During your ministerial journey your confidence must remain in the Lord. In spite of how intense the attacks of your enemies may become, do not be distracted by your enemy's poise. It is imperative that you do not respond until you have sought the Lord. 1 Chronicles 14:10 mentions how David inquired of God, saying, shall I go up against the Philistines? God will always provide you with strategies on how to handle your enemies.

Since David chose to depend on the infinite wisdom of the Lord, God not only destroyed David's enemy, but he destroyed his enemy's gods. (1 Chronicles 14:12) When you follow the anointing rest assured that God is fighting for you.

LESSON

1 Chronicles 14:1-17 ESV

I. Will cause favor to be released in your life

   A. Verse 1: "Now Hiram king of Tyre sent messengers to David, and timber of cedars, with masons and carpenters, to build him a house."

II. Your elevation is personable but not personal. It is for someone else and not about you.

   A. "David perceived that the Lord had confirmed him King over Israel" (**1 Chronicles 14:2a KJV**).

   B. "For his kingdom was lifted up on high because of his people Israel" (**1 Chronicles 14:2b KJV**)

   C. God had the people in mind more so than David. **II Samuel 5:12 KJV**, "And David perceived that the Lord had established him king over Israel, and that he had exalted his kingdom for his people Israel's sake."

III. When following the anointing, we must resist and subdue sensual desires because casual sin will tarnish your reputation.

    A. The first mistake David made was taking more wives and concubines.

    B. In Deuteronomy 17: 16 – 18 KJV: "But he shall not multiply horses to himself, nor cause the people to return to Egypt, to the end that he should multiply horses: forasmuch as the Lord hath said unto you, ye shall henceforth return no more that way. 17 Neither shall he multiply wives to himself, that his heart turn not away; neither shall he greatly multiply to himself silver and gold. 18 And it shall be, when he sitteth upon the throne of his kingdom, that he shall write him a copy of this law in a book out of that which is before the priest the Levites."

    C. God told him not to be multiplied in wives because they would lead his heart away from God.

    D. Do not multiply horses, women, silver and gold. Do not ever go or lead the people back into Egypt (**Deuteronomy 17:16 KJV**).

IV. Elevations and promotions are normally accompanied with new battles.

   A. When the Philistines heard that David was anointed king over all Israel, all the Philistines went up to see David. David heard of it and went out against them (I am not afraid).

V. Expect the enemy to make a grand show of force to test you.

   A. They "Spread themselves in the valley Rephaim", with their gods present (**1 Chronicles 14:9**).

   B. They position themselves as if they were saying, "come and get some."

   C. They were looking at David funny!

   D. Have people ever looked at you funny, staring you down as if they wanted to wage war on you?

   E. If your answer is yes, do not be distracted by your enemie's poise. Do not respond until you have sought God.

VI. Therefore, in times of uncertainty always seek God.

    A. **1 Chronicles 14:10 KJV**: "and David inquired of God, saying, shall I go up against the Philistines?

VII. Because you are capable does not mean that it is expedient to react or respond!

    A. "Wilt thou deliver them into mine hand?" (**1 Chronicles 14:10 KJV**) in other words, Lord I know my capabilities but what are you going to do?

    B. Some battles are not won by strength, ("Not by might, nor by power but by my Spirit saith the Lord of the hosts in") **Zechariah 4:6 KJV**

    C. Psalm **127:1 KJV**, "Except the LORD build the house, they labour in vain that build it: except the LORD keep the city, the watchman waketh but in vain."

VIII. When the battle is over and the victory has been gained, remember who fought and who gained.

    A. Song: Doc McKenzie "He Fought the Battle and I Won"

    B. **1 Chronicles 14:11 KJV,** "So came up to Baalperazim; and David smote them there. Then David said, God hath broken in upon mine enemies by mine hand like the breaking forth of waters: therefore they called the name of that place Baalperazim."

    C. Not only did God destroy David's enemy, but he destroyed his enemy's gods. **1 Chronicles 14:12 ESV**, "they left their gods there, (in the valley) and they (Israelites) burned them with fire", (by David's order).

IX. Satan is a repeat offender.

    A. **John 10:10 KJV**

    "The thief cometh not, but for to steal, and to kill, and to destroy: I am come that they might have life, and that they might have it more abundantly."

    B. **1 Chronicles 14:13 KJV**: "And the Philistines yet again spread themselves abroad in the valley."

- C. This time, no gods…not that they served any real purpose the last time.

X. Sometimes in order to defeat the enemy God will take you another way.

XI. "Therefore, David enquired again of God; and God said unto him, Go not up after them; turn away from them, and come upon them over against the mulberry trees" **(1 Chronicles 14:14 KJV).**

- A. 1 Chronicles 14:14a KJV, "Therefore, David <u>inquired again of God</u>; and God said unto him, Go not up after them: <u>turn away from them</u>.

Nugget: Sometimes you have to make it appear that you are ignoring your enemy in order for God to work!

- B. "And come upon them over against the mulberry trees" (1 Chronicles 14:14b)

- C. Do not move until God moves!

- D. 1 Chronicles 14:15 KJV: "And it shall be, when thou shalt hear a sound of going in the tops of the mulberry trees, that then thou shalt go out to battle: for God is gone forth before thee to smite the host of the Philistines."

E. That then thou shalt go out to battle for God has gone forth before thee to smite the host of the Philistines **(1Chronicles 14:15b)**

F. By following God, your victory will be certain.

G. **1 Chronicles 14:16a**, "David therefore did as God commanded him" (He totally followed God's voice).

H. "And they smote the host of the Philistines from Gibeon even to Gazer" (**1 Chronicles 14:16b)**

I. I heard Jehosaphat tell the people "Obey God."

Closing

I. Following the anointing will cause you to triumph in every place!

II. Following the anointing will cause you to leap over walls and run through a troop.

III. Will cause favor to be released in your life.

IV. Following the anointing, we must resist and subdue sensual desires.

V. In times of uncertainty seek God. **Jeremiah 33:3 KJV**, "Call unto me, and I will answer thee, and show thee great and mighty things, which thou knowest not."

VI. Some battles are not won by human might, nor by human power, but the Spirit of the Lord.

VII. "The LORD is my light and my salvation: whom shall I fear? The LORD is the strength of my life; of whom shall I be afraid" (**Psalm 27:1 KJV**)

VIII. "Wait on the Lord: be of good courage, and he shall strengthen thine heart: wait, I say on the Lord" (**Psalm 27:14 KJV**).

1. Chronicles 14:1-17 ESV

Now Hiram king of Tyre sent messengers to David, and timber of cedars, with masons and carpenters, to build him an house.

2. And David perceived that the Lord had confirmed him king over Israel, for his kingdom was lifted up on high, because of his people Israel.

3. And David took more wives at Jerusalem: and David begat more sons and daughters.

4. Now these are the names of his children which he had in Jerusalem; Shammua, and Shobab, Nathan, and Solomon,

5. And Ibhar, and Elishua, and Elpalet,

6. And Nogah, and Nepheg, and Japhia,

7. And Elishama, and Beeliada, and Eliphalet.

8. And when the Philistines heard that David was anointed king over all Israel, all the Philistines went up to seek David. And David heard of it, and went out against them.

9. And the Philistines came and spread themselves in the valley of Rephaim.

10. And David enquired of God, saying, Shall I go up against the Philistines? And wilt thou deliver them into mine hand? And the Lord said unto him, Go up; for I will deliver them into thine hand.

11. So they came up to Baalperazim; and David smote them there. Then David said, God hath broken in upon mine enemies by mine hand like the breaking forth of waters: therefore they called the name of that place Baalperazim.

12. And when they had left their gods there, David gave a commandment, and they were burned with fire.

13. And the Philistines yet again spread themselves abroad in the valley.

14. Therefore David enquired again of God; and God said unto him, Go not up after them; turn away from them, and come upon them over against the mulberry trees.

15. And it shall be, when thou shalt hear a sound of

going in the tops of the mulberry trees, that then thou shalt go out to battle: for God is gone forth before thee to smite the host of the Philistines.

16. David therefore did as God commanded him: and they smote the host of the Philistines from Gibeon even to Gazer.

17. And the fame of David went out into all lands; and the Lord brought the fear of him upon all nations.

Chapter 2
SELF EXAMINATION

Self-Examination

Leaders should live life in light of the saying: "There but for the grace of God, go I". In layman terms this simply means: the bad situations that you may know others to be in, could be you if it had not been for God's grace. Essentially this saying sums up the importance of not being quick to judge someone by their shortcomings and downfalls. Truth be told we all have them. Therefore, the focus of a leader should much more be inward than outward.

Self examination should be a primary responsibility of every leader. It keeps one in a place of humility and shields you from falling subject to a critical spirit. Jesus taught against a judgmental attitude that tears down in order to build oneself up. God is more concerned with censoriousness, which is the spirit of fault finding that overlooks one's own shortcomings and at the same time assuming the role of supreme judge in regards to the sins of other people.

In Matthew 7:1-6 Jesus provides the blueprint for judging. When Jesus says "judge not" this refers to condemnatory judgment. It doesn't explicitly mean that a Christian should never exercise judgment of any kind under any given circumstances. The greater point that we should grasp here is that we are not to judge the inner motives of another. In fact we don't have the insight to do so. The only person that will ever know exactly why someone would do the things they do is God. Therefore, we are not to render a verdict based on prejudice information.

Jesus also instructs that we should not use ourselves as the standard of judgment. The measure we use to judge others, will in fact be the same measure we are judged. The ultimate judgment will not be our own judgment but the judgment of God.

Keeping in step with the way Christ calls us to judge also shields us from being hypocritical and self righteous. We must be deliberate about not condemning others for their small fault (mote), yet overlooking our own great fault (beam). Metaphorically speaking a mote is a small speck of sawdust. On the other hand a beam is a rafter used in building. It is virtually impossible and hypocritical to attempt to remove the speck from your brother/sister's eye until you have removed the rafter from your own eye.

We have been granted the authority to judge, but are to do so the way God instructs us in His Word. There are circumstances as leaders in which we are to exercise church discipline and trust God to be the final judge. We see this type of church discipline mentioned in several of the epistles written by the Apostle Paul.

One being 2 Corinthians 2:5 KJV, "But if any have caused grief, he hath not grieved me, but in part: that I may not overcharge you all." Simply put the Apostle Paul was saying that if someone has caused grief in the assembly, the offense is not so much against the apostle as it is the local assembly. Therefore, the obligation of discipline was not of the apostle but the responsibility of the leadership of the local church. Leaders in God's house are charged to exercise church discipline. The difference maker is in doing so free of a self righteous & hypocritical approach, showing mercy, and trusting God to be the final judge.

LESSON

MATTHEW 7:1-6

I. Is there a place for criticism, opinions, or condemnation of wrong doing?

II. Could the issue be that God is more concerned with censoriousness, which is the spirit of fault finding that overlooks one's own shortcomings and at the same time assuming the role of supreme judge in regard to the sins of other people? Jesus taught against judgmental attitude that tear down in order to build oneself up.

III. Could it be that God calls us to be discerning and not negative in our thinking process (**Matthew 7:15-23**)? "Beware" (**1 Corinthians 5:1-2**).

We are to exercise church discipline, and trust God to be the final judge (**1 Corinthians 4:3-5**).

Matthew 7:15-23 KJV: 15 Beware of false prophets, which come to you in sheep's clothing, but inwardly they are ravening wolves. 16 Ye shall know them by their fruits. Do men gather grapes of thorns, or figs of thistles? 17 Even so every good tree bringeth forth good fruit; but a corrupt tree bringeth forth evil fruit. 18 A good tree cannot bring forth evil fruit, neither can a corrupt tree bring forth good fruit. 19 Every tree that bringeth not forth good fruit is hewn down and cast into the fire. 20 Wherefore by their fruits ye shall know them. 21 Not everyone that saith unto me, Lord, Lord, shall enter into the kingdom of heaven; but he that doeth the will of my Father which is in heaven. 22 Many will say to me in that day, Lord, Lord, have we not prophesied in thy name? and in thy name have cast out devils? and in thy name done many wonderful works? 23 And then will I profess unto them, I never knew you: depart from me, ye that work iniquity.

1. **1 Corinthians 5:1-2 KJV**; "It is reported commonly that there is fornication among you, and such fornication as is not so much as named among the Gentiles, that one should have his father's wife."

2. "And ye are puffed up, and have not rather mourned, that he that hath done this deed might be taken away from among you."

3. **1 Corinthians 4:3-5 KJV,** " But with me it is a very small thing that I should be judged of you, or of man's judgment: yea, I judge not mine own self.

4. "For I know nothing by myself; yet am I not hereby justified: but he that judgeth me is the Lord."

5. "Therefore judge nothing before the time, until the Lord come, who both will bring to light the hidden things of darkness, and will make manifest the counsels of the hearts: and then shall every man have praise of God."

VI. Could it be that the Christian is to judge certain matters, but not hypocritically or self-righteously (**1 Thessalonians 5:12 KJV** "prove all things; hold fast to that which is good". The Bible asks us to follow these steps in order to determine one's spiritual placement.

    A. Examine yourself. Examine your own motives and conduct. Many times the traits that bother us and other people are often the habits we dislike in ourselves. In other words, we see ourselves. Do we magnify others faults in order to ignore our own faults?

    B. **2 Corinthians 2:5 KJV**:

But if any have caused grief, he hath not grieved me, but in part: that I may not overcharge you all.
Examine yourselves as to whether you are in the faith. Correct personal faults and solve your own problems before attempting to correct faults and other people. Let any judgemental attitude in yourself signal the need to examine yourself for things that bother you about others.

    C. **Galatians 6:3-4 KJV**:

For if a man think himself to be something, when he is nothing, he deceiveth himself.

⁴ But let every man prove his own work, and then shall he have rejoicing in himself alone, and not in another.

D. Evaluate people's character rather than their being.

V. Could it be that God wants us to discern a person's spiritual placement in order to bring them into forgiveness?

Luke 6:36-38 KJV

³⁶ Be ye therefore merciful, as your Father also is merciful.

³⁷ Judge not, and ye shall not be judged: condemn not, and ye shall not be condemned: forgive, and ye shall be forgiven:

³⁸ Give, and it shall be given unto you; good measure, pressed down, and shaken together, and running over, shall men give into your bosom. For with the same measure that ye mete withal it shall be measured to you again.

Luke 6:36-38 (KJV)

³⁶ Be ye therefore merciful, as your Father is merciful.

Look at Yourselves

37 "Don't judge others, and you will not be judged. Don't accuse others of being guilty, and you will not be accused of being guilty. Forgive, and you will be forgiven.

38 Give, and you will receive. You will be given much. Pressed down, shaken together, and running over, it will spill into your lap. The way you give to others is the way God will give to you."

IV. Finally, **Matthew 7:6:** Jesus taught that doctrine should be given in accordance with spiritual capacity on the learner. We must first discern what level a person is on. In the text, Jesus used dogs, swine, and false prophets.

Matthew 7:6 KJV "Give not that which is holy unto dogs, neither cast ye your pearls before swine, lest they trample them under their feet, and turn again and rend you."

   A. Street dogs were held in low self-esteem and considered unclean.

   B. Swine were unclean animals according to God's Law (**Deuteronomy 14:8),** Anyone who touched an unclean animal became "ceremonially unclean" and could not go to the temple to worship. Do not entrust holy teachings to unholy or unclean people. It is futile to try to teach holy concepts to people who do not want to listen and will only tear apart that which we say.

Deuteronomy 14:8 KJV: "And the swine, because it divideth the hoof, yet cheweth not the cud, it is unclean unto you: ye shall not eat of their flesh nor touch their dead carcase."

C. However, this does not mean that we should stop spreading God's Word to unbelievers but that we should exercise wisdom and discernment in our teaching process, so that we are not wasting our time. We must redeem time because time is short and the days are evil.

Chapter 3
GOD'S REQUIRED ACTION PLAN FOR SPIRITUAL LEADERSHIP

God's Required Action Plan for Spiritual Leadership

Many people often ask the question, "What should be the primary focus of a spiritual leader?" Contrary to popular belief it's not the cultivation of your gift. Much rather it is the word of God. The word of God should be the primary focus of a spiritual leader. Spiritual leaders must have a disciplined study life of God's Word. The scripture in 2 Timothy 2:15 says, "Study to shew thyself approved unto God, a workman that needeth not to be ashamed, rightly dividing the word of truth".

The only way to healthy, balanced living is through the "rightly dividing" (Greek orthotomeo literally cutting straight) of God's Word; which is correct, straight-on application of God's Word which comes as a result of diligent study. This requires more than a casual approach to scriptures; therefore, we cannot use the Bible for convenience. As spiritual leaders we should not only be in our word for the purpose of preaching. We are called to be in our word for personal edification above all else. A great study life is paramount in the life of a healthy spiritual leader.

David in Psalm 119:11 KJV states, "Thy word have I hid in mine heart, that I might not sin against thee." David had to toil and put forth effort to memorize the Word of God as a mighty deterrent against sin. The word of God hidden in our heart due to our diligent study is the greatest way we combat sin.

Memorizing the word of God is an essential part of studying the word of God. Memorizing the scripture also provides an immediate availability of God's "words" as a sword, ready in witnessing and effective in spiritual warfare. The word of God is a powerful weapon.

We are to use the Word in faith, believing that there is no inerrancy in the scripture, there's no private interpretation, and all scripture was given by inspiration of God. 2 Timothy 3:16 KJV says: "All scripture is given by the inspiration of God, and is profitable for doctrine, for reproof, for correction, for instruction in righteousness". "For doctrine" meaning it will teach us truth and cause us to realize wrongs in our life, "for reproof" meaning it will convict you, convince you, rebuke, it will tell your faults, "for correction" meaning it will reform and rectify, it will provide spiritual relocation for those who are displaced and "for instruction", (tutorage, education, training) in "righteousness."

Meditating on the Word of God is something we are instructed to do day and night. Joshua 1:8 mentions how it is a pivotal part of success and prosperity in God.

Aside from the word of God being the primary focus of a spiritual leader there are several other components to God's required action plan for spiritual leadership. These other components are not intended to be the end all be all.

One being the importance of praying for the voice of God to inspire both your conscious and unconscious thoughts. Philippians 4:8 instructs us of what we are to spend our time thinking upon. "Finally, brethren, whatsoever things are <u>true</u>, whatsoever things are <u>honest</u>, whatsoever things are <u>just</u>, whatsoever things are <u>pure</u>, whatsoever things are <u>lovely</u>, whatsoever things are of

<u>good report</u>; if there be any virtue, and if there be any <u>praise</u>, think on these things." We should pray earnestly that the Father teaches us to think on things that are virtuous and praise worthy.

Additionally, spiritual leaders should practice the spiritual disciplines of guarding their heart (Proverbs 4:23), forgiving as often as needed (Matthew 18:21-22), praying in the Holy Ghost (Jude 1:20), and keeping themselves in the love of God. (Jude 1:21).

LESSON

I. First and foremost a disciplined study life of God's Word.

    A. A. **2 Timothy 2:15 KJV:** "Study to show thyself approved unto God, a workman that needeth not ashamed, rightly dividing the word of truth.

    B. The only way to healthy, balanced living is through the "rightly dividing" (Greek orthotomeo literally "cutting straight") of God's Word; which is correct, straight-on application of God's Word which comes as a result of diligent study. This requires more than a casual approach to scriptures; therefore we cannot use the Bible for convenience.

    C. Study: (Greek ergon-"toil, effort") **Psalms 119:11 KJV,** "Thy word have I hid in mine heart, that I might not sin against thee.

        1. David had to toil and put forth effort to memorize the Word of God as a mighty deterrent against sin.

        2. Long term memory, short term memory recall.

D. Memorizing the scripture also provides an immediate availability of God's "words" as a sword, ready in witnessing and effective in spiritual warfare.

E. Use the Word in faith, believing that there is no inerrancy in the scripture. No private interpretation and that all scripture was given by inspiration of God.

> 1. **2 Timothy 3:16 KJV:** "All scripture is given by the inspiration of God, and is profitable for doctrine", (it will teach us truth and cause us to realize wrongs in our life) "for reproof" (it will convict you, convince you, rebuke, it will tell your faults) "for correction", (it will reform and rectify, it will provide spiritual relocation for those who are displaced) "for instruction", (tutorage, education, training) in "righteousness."

> 2. **2 Timothy 3:17 KJV:** "That the man of God may be perfect," (reek aritos, ar'-tee-os; fresh complete) "thoroughly furnished unto all good works" (fully equipped, as a

fully accomplished teacher).

F. **John 8:31-32 KJV,** 31 Then said Jesus to the Jews which believed on him, If ye continue in my word, then are ye my disciples indeed; 32 And ye shall know the truth and the truth shall make you free. (liberate you; exempt you from the bondage of sin).

G. Meditate on the Word, **Joshua 1:8 KJV,** "This <u>book</u> of the law shall not depart out of thy <u>mouth</u>; but thou <u>shall meditate</u> there in <u>day</u> and <u>night</u>, that thou mayest observe to do according to all that is written there in: for then thou shalt make thy <u>way</u> prosperous and then thou <u>shalt have good success</u>."

   1. Information
   2. Saturation (knowledge and understanding)
   3. Application (wisdom)

Secondly,

A.   Pray for the voice of God to inspire your thought.

B.   Conscious and unconscious thoughts (sleep).

C.   **Philippians 4:8 KJV,** "Finally, brethren, whatsoever things are <u>true</u>, whatsoever things are <u>honest</u>, whatsoever things are <u>just</u>, whatsoever things are <u>pure</u>, whatsoever things are <u>lovely</u>, whatsoever things are of <u>good report</u>; if there be any virtue, and if there be any <u>praise</u>, think on these things."

D.   **Proverbs 4:23 KJV,** "Keep thy heart with all diligence; for out of it are issues of life.

   *NOTE: Above all, we should value and protect our mind, will, and emotions.

   *NOTE: Diligence, careful effort, perseverance, persistence, and steadfastness.

II. Additionally

A. Forgive as often as needed.

B. **Matthew 6:12 KJV,** "And forgive us our debts, as we forgive our debtors. (**Matthew 18:22 KJV,** "Jesus saith unto him, I say not unto thee, Until seven times: but, Until seventy times seven").

III. Next

A. Build your faith by praying in the Holy Ghost.

B. **Jude 1:20 KJV,** "But ye, beloved, building up yourselves on your most holy faith, praying in the Holy Ghost,"

III. Finally

A. Keep yourself in the love of God and repent as often as needed.

B. **Jude 1:21 KJV,** "Keep yourselves in the love of God, looking for the mercy of our Lord Jesus Christ into eternal life."

C. **Acts 3:19 KJV,** "Repent ye therefore and be converted, that your sins may be blotted out, when the times of refreshing shall come from the presence of the Lord."

IV. In Closing, please remember to:
   A. Stay with the Basics. **2 Timothy 3:14 KJV:** "But continue thou in the things which thou hast learned and hast been assured of, knowing of whom thou hast learned them;

   B. Put the Word in long term memory.
   C. Study.
   D. Memorize.
   E. Meditate.
   F. Pray for God's voice to inspire your thoughts
   G. Guard your heart.
   H. Forgive.
   I. Pray in the Holy Ghost.
   J. Keep yourself in the love of God.

Chapter 4
SEVENFOLD PURPOSE OF THE PASTOR

Sevenfold Purpose of the Pastor

The purpose of a pastor from a biblical viewpoint far exceeds preaching sermons on Sundays and teaching bible studies during the week. There are seven aspects of the purpose of the pastor that I will be honing in on here. Prayerfully you'll gain greater insight on how vast the responsibility of a pastor is by God's design.

Ephesians 4:12-13 discloses several aspects of the purpose of a pastor. It says: "For the perfecting of the saints, for the work of the ministry, for the edifying of the body of Christ:

Till we all come in the unity of the faith, and of the knowledge of the Son of God, unto a perfect man, unto the measure of the stature of the fullness of Christ". The responsibility of the pastor is the perfecting of the saints, that is to train and equip Christians to do the work of the ministry. The ultimate aim of the pastor equipping other believers for ministry is for the sole purpose of edifying the body of Christ in order to build up the church numerically and spiritually. There's nothing wrong with growth in numbers as long as the emphasis of growth is much more on the spiritual growth of the people you are called to shepherd. The edifying of the church is to continue till we all come in the unity of the faith. Meaning until all Christians attain spiritual maturity. Due to the fact that new believers are constantly being added to the church, this goal will not be realized until the Lord returns

Pastors are called to feed the sheep with knowledge and understanding according to Jeremiah 3:15 KJV which states: " And I will give you pastors according to mine heart, which shall feed you with knowledge and understanding." This knowledge and understanding can be better explained as Dhe ah- knowledge; what one knows, wisdom, to be familiar, to be informed and Sakhal- understanding; to be circumspect, be prudent, skill, expertise, be intelligent, to have insight, pay attention, intellectual comprehension. Sakhal relates to an intelligent knowledge of reason for something.

Pastors after God's own heart understand that it is vitally important to serve under the Great Shepherd Himself.

Jeremiah 23:2 KJV emphasizes that pastors are to visit the flock. "Therefore thus saith the Lord God of Israel against the pastors that feed my people: Ye have scattered my flock, and driven them away, and have not visited them: behold, I will visit upon you the evil of your doings, saith the LORD."

To visit (paquad) means to inspect, review; to muster, number, to care for, and look after. Paquad is a positive action by a superior in relation to his subordinates. Judgment from God will be granted to those who have scattered and driven away God's flock. The heart of a pastor that has God's agenda in mind for his people, make it their duty to care for them.

In addition to visiting the flock, the purpose of the pastor is to feed the flock. Feeding includes the totality of the office of the shepherd. A pastor ultimately is responsible for the guarding, guiding, folding of the flock as well as leading it to nourishment. (See 1Peter 5:2)

Lastly, a pastor is to be examples to the flock. Of course , above all else we are to follow in the footsteps of Jesus. He should be the supreme example in the life of the believer. However, according to 1 Peter 5:3 "Neither as being lords over God's heritage, but being examples to the flock" pastors are a prototype of what is to be developed and evolved.

Definition of terms: The Greek word episkopos designates a local Pastoral oversight. It is derived from monarchical episcopate as the title of Bishop. To better express the meaning of the word, "supervisor" or "overseers" are comparable in meaning. The word also may be referred to as "Presbyter" or "Elder" making referenced to the same office.

LESSON

1. The sevenfold purpose of Pastors from a biblical viewpoint.

    A. For the perfecting of the saints: (Ephesians 4:13) Completeness- aid in finishing the work of Christ through the word.

    Ephesians 4:13 KJV:
    "Till we all come in the unity of the faith, and of the knowledge of the Son of God, unto a perfect man, unto the measure of the stature of the fullness of Christ."

    Maturity-growth, stability, integrity

    Equipping- katartismos (kat-ar-tis-moss) a making fit, preparing, training, making fully qualified for service.

    The Greek word (katartismos) implies a recovered wholeness as when a broken bone is set and mends. Also discovered function, as when a physical member is properly operating.

B. For the work of the ministry.

Preparing the saints for the work of the ministry to cultivate the individuals that he or she leads and to cultivate the corporate ministries of those he or she leads.

C. For the edifying of the Body of Christ.

Building up and internal strengthening.

NOTE: External provides the look and internal provides the method.

D. Feed the sheep with <u>knowledge and understanding.</u>

Jeremiah 3:15 KJV: " And I will give you pastors according to mine heart, which shall feed you with knowledge and understanding."

Dhe ah-knowledge; what one knows, wisdom, to be familiar, to be informed.

Sakhal- understanding; to be circumspect, be prudent, skill, expertise, be intelligent, to have insight, pay attention, intellectual comprehension. Sakhal relates to an intelligent knowledge of reason for something.

E. To <u>visit</u> the flock.

Jeremiah 23:2 KJV: "Therefore thus saith the Lord God of Israel against the pastors that feed my people: Ye have scattered my flock, and driven them away, and have not visited them: behold, I will visit upon you the evil of your doings, saith the LORD."

Visit (paquad)- inspect, review; to muster, number, to care for, and look after. Paquad is a positive action by a superior in relation to his subordinates.

F. To feed the flock of God (I Peter 5:2).

Feed (poimaino)- shepherd, tend; it implies the whole office of the shepherd. Guarding, guiding, folding of the flock as well as leading it to nourishment.

Acts 20:28 KJV: "Take heed therefore unto yourselves, and to all the flock, over which the Holy Ghost hath made you <u>overseers, to feed</u> the Church of God, which hath purchased with his own blood."

(Oversight- look upon, observe, look after, and examine).

To be examples to the flock. A prototype of that is to be developed and evolved.

I Peter 5:3 KJV: "Neither as being lords over God's heritage, but being examples to the flock."

Chapter 5
Teamwork Makes the Dream Work

Teamwork Makes the Dream Work

Many times, in life God assigns various leaders to specified regions with a divine mission. That mission may seem burdensome, heavy, and maybe even impossible. Nonetheless, God will provide a team to aid in the matter at hand. Working together will make it happen.

In fact, team ministry is a part of God's plan for effectiveness and efficiency. There are countless examples in the bible of teams orchestrated by God for the work of the Lord. The saying: " no man is an island" is applicable concerning ministry also. We get much more accomplished when we're on one accord working towards God's agenda.

The truth of the matter is that service to God oftentimes comes with a burden. Many pastors experience burn out due to them carrying the load of ministry by themselves. Being one called and chosen to be a pastor does have its privileges. However, those on the outside looking in tend to overlook the great responsibilities associated with the call. This is why team work is of paramount importance. I believe pastors should seek the Lord concerning being strategic about setting up teams to help carry the load of ministry, much rather than doing everything themselves. Quite frankly it's a recipe for disaster not to.

A great biblical example of the benefits of having a strong support system is that of Moses in Exodus 17:12. Which says: "But Moses hands were heavy; and they took a stone, and put it under him, and he sat thereon; and Aaron and Hur stayed up his hands, the one on the one side, and the other on the other side; and his hands were steady until the going down of the sun."

Moses had grown weary physically. His hands, stretched to heaven, became heavy to the point that he could no longer raise them up, nor stretch them out, by his own muscular strength. Both of his hands dropped down by his sides. If this battle he was up against was to be won, a remedy needed to take place. Here's where the blessing of having a great team came into play. The leadership team of Moses, Aaron (the high priest) and Hur (the armor bearer) came up with an effective remedy. They took a stone which provided Moses with rest and enabled them to better sustain his hands.

With the help of Aaron and Hur the once mentally and bodily exhausted Moses, was sustained physically by his two companions apart of his team. Moses was therefore able to recover mentally also, which enabled him to renew his supplications that he had been too weak to continue with previously. He had ceased to pray due to his exhaustion. The beauty of the story is that since Aaron and Hur stepped in and assisted their leader the victory was won.

The success of your ministry work as a pastor or leader alike is contingent upon the strength and assistance of those working alongside of you. What we learn from Moses is that he was glad of the help he received from Aaron and Hur. He humbly accepted the remedy they came up with to aid in the victory of the battle. As leaders it is important the we do the same. We should not be opposed to asking for help from those that God has strategically placed in our lives for the work of the ministry. The will of the Lord is accomplished when we come together on one accord to fulfill a corporate mission. Team work does truly make the dream work.

LESSON

I. **Exodus 17:12 KJV:** "But Moses hands were heavy; and they took a stone, and put it under him, and he sat thereon; and Aaron and Hur stayed up his hands, the one on the side, and the other on the other side; and his hands were steady until the going down of the sun."

II. **Psalms 34:9 KJV:** "Many are the afflictions of the righteous: But the LORD delivereth him out of them all." Paul stated all they that live godly shall suffer (persecution).

III. Service to God many times comes with a burden.

    A. The Pastor carries the load.
    B. RHIP (Rank Has Its Privileges) as well as its responsibilities.
    C. God is concerned about all our daily activities.

    D. **Acts 17:28 KJV:** "For in him we live, and move, and have our being; as certain also of your own poets have said, For we are also his offspring."

E. **Matthew 11:28 KJV:** "Come unto me, all ye that labour and heavy laden, and I will give you rest."

Nonetheless, lift up your head.

A. David said in **Psalms 24:7-9 KJV**: "Lift up your hands, O ye gates; and be ye lift up, ye everlasting doors; and the King of glory shall come in. 8 Who is this King of glory? The Lord strong and mighty, the Lord mighty in battle. 9 Lift up your heads, O ye gates; even lift them up, ye everlasting doors; and the King of glory shall come in."

B. **Exodus 17:8-16 KJV:** 8 Then came Amalek, and fought with Israel in Rephidim.

IV. And Moses said unto Joshua, Choose us out men, and go out, fight with Amalek: to morrow I will stand on the top of the hill with the rod of God in mine hand.

V. So Joshua did as Moses had said to him, and fought with Amalek: and Moses, Aaron, and Hur went up to the top of the hill.

VI. And it came to pass, when Moses held up his

hand, that Israel prevailed: and when he let down his hand, Amalek prevailed.

VII. But Moses' hands were heavy; and they took a stone, and put it under him, and he sat thereon; and Aaron and Hur stayed up his hands, the one on the one side, and the other on the other side; and his hands were steady until the going down of the sun.

VIII. And Joshua discomfited Amalek and his people with the edge of the sword.

IX. And the Lord said unto Moses, Write this for a memorial in a book, and rehearse it in the ears of Joshua: for I will utterly put out the remembrance of Amalek from under heaven.

X. And Moses built an altar, and called the name of it Jehovah-nissi:

XI. For he said, Because the Lord hath sworn that the Lord will have war with Amalek from generation to generation.

C. Moses-Leadership
- Aaron-High Priest
- Joshua-Warning servant (God slaves)
- Hur- Armor Bearer

    1. Be encouraged. Victory today is yours.

    2. Be strong in the Lord.

    3. They that wait on the Lord shall renew their strength.

    4. Even though your laughter has been turned into mourning.

    5. Weeping may endure for a night…

    6. Keep trusting in the Lord, some trust in chariots..

Chapter 6
TOGETHER WE CAN

Together We Can

Much more can be accomplished for the Lord when we are unified as brothers and sisters in Christ. We can do more with other Christians who have the same burden. The definition of unity is oneness of mind, feeling, etc. To be unified is to be in harmony, or agreement. Psalm 133:1 says "Behold, how good and how pleasant it is for brethren to dwell together in unity!"

God desires that we live amongst each other free of quarrelling yet unified. To be truly unified is to dwell as one. Having one heart, one soul, and one interest. Simply put, being on one accord across the board. It's important to note that being unified does not mean disagreements will not occur. However, learning to agree to disagree should never prohibit us from moving forth in the corporate mission.

In fact this kind of committed unity enables us to fight against the enemy at a greater magnitude. There are countless scriptures in the bible that give credence to the fact that together our impact is substantial. (See Joshua 23:10, Deuteronomy 32:30-37)

True impact is not predicated upon numbers more than it is a group of people that are sincerely united. The bible talks about "And five of you shall chase an hundred, and an hundred of you shall put ten thousand to flight: and your enemies shall fall before you by the sword." - Leviticus 26:8.

This scripture is a proverbial expression signifying that a very few, under Divine providence, should get the advantage over a large number. God is in our midst when we are unified. Unity is key to having victory over the enemy. Many leaders put a lot of attention on establishing a big ministry. Growth in number is good. However, it is possible for a ministry to be large in number yet unhealthy. The true health of the ministry the Lord has called you to lies in the unity amongst the people.

The truth that many leaders are in dire need of is that the enemy does not fear a big church. The enemy fears a united church. When a church is united much more can get accomplished for God's glory. United we can win the lost. United we can cast out more demons. United we can experience the move of God. United we can increase the quality of life for others. Together we are better.

LESSON

MARK 9:38-41 (KJV)

38 And John answered him, saying, Master, we saw one casting out devils in thy name, and he followeth not us: and we forbad him, because he followeth not us.

39 But Jesus said, Forbid him not: for there is no man which shall do a miracle in my name, that can lightly speak evil of me.

40 For he that is not against us is on our part.

41 For whosoever shall give you a cup of water to drink in my name, because ye belong to Christ, verily I say unto you, he shall not lose his reward.

I. A Message of Unity

Psalm 133 (KJV)

133 Behold, how good and how pleasant it is for brethren to dwell together in unity!

² It is like the precious ointment upon the head, that ran down upon the beard, even Aaron's beard: that went down to the skirts of his garments;

³ As the dew of Hermon, and as the dew that descended upon the mountains of Zion: for there the Lord commanded the blessing, even life forevermore.

Philippians 4:13 KJV: "I can do all things through Christ which strengthens me."

A. But I can do more with other Christians who have the same burden.

Joshua 23:10 KJV: "One man of you shall chase a thousand: for the Lord your God, he it is that fighteth for you, as he hath promised you."

Leviticus 26:8 KJV: "And five of you shall chase an hundred, and a hundred of you shall put ten thousand to flight: and your enemies shall fall before you by the sword."

Deuteronomy 32:30-37 KJV: How should one chase a thousand, and two put ten thousand to flight, except their Rock had sold them, and the Lord had shut them up? For their rock is not as our Rock, even our enemies themselves being judges. For their vine is of the vine of Sodom, and of the fields of Gomorrah: their grapes are grapes of gall, their clusters are bitter: Their wine is the poison of dragons, and the cruel venom of asps. Is not this laid up in store with me, and sealed up among my treasures? To me belongeth vengeance, and recompense; their foot shall slide in due time: for the day of their calamity is at hand, and the things that shall come upon them make haste.

For the Lord shall judge his people, and repent himself for his servants, when he seeth that their power is gone, and there is none shut up, or left. And he shall say, Where are their gods, their rock in whom they trusted,"

II. TOGETHER WE CAN!

Peter and John at the Hour of Prayer

Acts 3:1-10 KJV: "Now Peter and John went up together into the temple at the hour of prayer, being the ninth hour. 2 And a certain man lame from his mother's womb was carried, whom they laid daily at the gate of the temple which is called Beautiful, to ask alms of them that entered in to the temple; 3 Who seeing Peter and John about to go into the temple asked an alms. 4 And Peter, fastening his eyes upon him with John, said, Look on us. 5 And he gave heed unto them, expecting to receive something of them. 6 Then Peter said, Silver and gold have I none; but such as I have given thee: In the name of Jesus Christ of Nazareth rise up and walk. 7 And he took him by the right hand, and lifted him up: and immediately his feet and ankle bones received strength. 8 And he leaping up stood, and walked, and entered with them into the temple, walking and praising God: 10 And they knew that it was he which sat for alms at the Beautiful gate of the temple: and they were filled with wonder and amazement at that which had happened unto him.

1. Win the lost.
2. Do more. Cast out more demons.
3. Experience the move of God. One accord (Acts 2).
4. Do better: We can increase the quality of life for others.

Mark 2:1-5 KJV: "And again He entered into Capernaum after some days; and it was noised that he was in the house. 2 And straightway many were gathered together, insomuch that there was no room to receive them, no, not so much as about the door; and he preached the word unto them. 3 And they come unto him, bringing one sick of the palsy, which was borne of four. 4 And when they could not come nigh unto him for the press they uncovered the roof where he was; and when they had broken it up, they let down the bed wherein the sick of palsy lay. 5 When Jesus saw their faith, he said unto the sick of palsy, Son, thy sins be forgiven thee."

Chapter 7
A Legacy of Influence: Leaving Your Mark

A Legacy of Influence: Leaving your Mark!

It is God's desire that when we depart this life and have a relationship with Jesus that we leave behind a legacy. One of the most influential ways we can leave a legacy is by being one who exudes the image of Christ. This is done by operating in our authoritative gifts passed down by God for the purpose of strengthening the body of Christ, and by walking in the character of a Kingdom citizen.

In Ephesians 4:8 it says, that when Jesus Christ ascended up on high, He led captivity captive, and gave gifts unto men. These gifts were for the perfecting of the saints. Being one who is instrumental in the development of the spiritual maturity of others leaves a lasting mark in their lives.

The character of a Christian is oftentimes the most impressionable. It is not enough to just be gifted alone, but we are called to be living witnesses. The Beatitudes in Matthew 5 describe the essential character of Kingdom citizens. Each beatitude includes a pronouncement of blessing, a description of the ones considered as blessed and an explanation for the blessing. Blessed means "happy". It is a grace word that expresses the special joy and satisfaction granted the person who experiences salvation. The beatitudes were taught by Jesus in the Sermon on the Mount. The life of the believer described by Jesus is a life of grace and glory, which comes from God alone. Throughout the Beatitudes Jesus clearly mentions that only those who have the qualities of a changed life, as described, are citizens of His kingdom. (See Matthew 5:1-12)

The Beatitudes are followed by a summary statement of the basic character of the Christian's life as salt and light. In verses 13-16 of Matthew 5, Jesus uses the metaphor of salt and light to indicate the kingdom citizen's influence for good as they penetrate secular society. Those who are genuinely born again are the salt and can help meet the needs of the world. Salt adds flavoring, acts as a preservative, melts coldness, and heals wounds. In addition, the essential mission of the Christian is to be the light of the world. Our light is to clearly shine forth into the darkness of human depravity.

When we walk in our rightful position as the salt and light we serve as an influence to many. Enhancing the lives of many people by providing advice, leadership, direction, discipline, and support to all we come in contact with is how we leave our mark for Jesus here in the earth.

LESSON

A Legacy of Influence: Leaving your Mark!

MATTHEW 5:13-16

In Ephesians 4:8, that when Jesus Christ ascended or in high, He led captivity captive, and gave gifts unto men for the perfecting of the saints. He passes down authoritative gifts that have served to strengthen the Body of Christ. Most of the people who depart this life and have a relationship with Jesus leave behind a legacy.

Ephesians 4:8 KJV: "Wherefore he saith, when he ascended on high, he led captivity captive, and gave gifts unto men."

I. The Beatitudes describe the essential character of Kingdom citizens:

II. Matthew 3:12 KJV:

"whose fan is in his hand, and he will thoroughly purge his floor, and gather his wheat into the garner; but he will burn up the chaff with unquenchable fire."

- A. Blessed- (mak-ar-ee-oss) derived from the root mak, indicating large or of long duration. The word is an adjective suggesting happy, supremely, a condition in which congratulations are in order.

- B. It is a grace word that expresses the special joy and satisfaction granted the person who experiences salvation.

- C. Each beatitude includes a pronouncement of blessing, a description of the ones considered at blessed and an explanation for the blessing.

- D. The poor in spirit: are those who recognize their spiritual poverty, casting aside all self-dependence seek God's grace.

- E. The who mourn: Are not necessarily people in bereavement but those who experience the sorrow of repentance.

F. Meek: controlled strength. The word carries the idea of humility and self-discipline.

G. Hunger and thirsty all righteousness

H. Merciful: Those who have an active desire to remove the cause of distress in others. They show kindness and concern for someone in serious need.

I. Pure in Heart: speaking the truth in your heart (as a man think it in his heart).

J. Peacemakers: called the sons of God. God is the supreme peacemaker and his sons follow His example.

K. Persecuted for righteousness sake: the cause of the persecution is loyalty to righteousness. To the point that when people rival and persecute you, and say all kinds of evil against you falsely for my namesake. Rejoice! Be exceedingly glad, for great is your reward in heaven.

III. Now in verses 13-16, Jesus uses the metaphor of salt and light to indicate the kingdom citizens influence for good as they penetrate secular society.

    A. Both salt a light have influence.

    B. Salt enhances the flavor of various foods calling them to take better (more up easy to The taste bud).

    C. Light provides a way out of darkness. It provides illumination into darkness and lightens the way or path.

    D. Some saints are both salt and light.

        1. They enhance the lives of many other people.

        2. They enhance, epitomize class, and perfection by example.

        3. They possess godly lifestyles which serve and influence to many.

        4. They shine very bright with love and kindness that there is no way they can go unnoticed. Matthew 5:15 KJV: "neither do me light a candle and put it under a bushel, but on a candlestick; and it giveth light unto all that

are in the house." A lamp or a lampstand gives light to all who are in the house, whether you want it or not.

5. Children of light give advice, leadership, direction, discipline, in support to all they come in contact with.

Matthew 5:16 KJV: "let your light so shine before men, that they may see your good works, and glorify your father which is in heaven." God's children allow their life to shine. They do their part in Kingdom building and aiding to equip others saints.

    A. Press for the mark.

    B. Get your well done.

    C. Fight the good fight of faith and receive your crowns of righteousness.

    D. The songwriter, R. H. Cornelius wrote:

Oh, I want to see Him, look upon His face,
There to sing forever of His saving grace;
On the streets of glory let me lift my voice,
Cares all past, home at last, ever to rejoice.

E. The songwriter, Eliza E. Hewitt wrote:

> **When we all get to heaven,**
>
> **What a day of rejoicing that will be!**
>
> **When we all see Jesus,**
>
> **We'll sing and shout the victory!**

F. Traveling shoes, I've got on my traveling shoes.

> **I can travel on now. I've got on my traveling shoes.**

G. The songwriter Ernest W. Blandly wrote:

> **I can hear my Savior calling,**
>
> **I can hear my Savior calling,**
>
> **I can hear my Savior calling,**
>
> **"Take thy cross and follow, follow Me."**

H. Oh, I am determined to walk with Jesus. Yes, I am.

> **Through hard trials, tribulations, and persecutions; I will**
>
> **Be faithful! I am determined to walk with Jesus, yes I am!**

ABOUT THE AUTHOR
Bishop Lorenzo N. Peterson

Archbishop Lorenzo N. Peterson is the Founder and Emeritus of the New Hope Freedom and Deliverance Cathedral in Louisburg, North Carolina. Archbishop Peterson is a husband and father, married to the beautiful Starlett Watson-Peterson of Tacoma, Washington. Archbishop Peterson initially received his ministerial training from the Burgaw Minister's Institute under the direction of his father, Rev.

Robert F. Peterson Sr. at age 14. Later, he was licensed in the ministry under the leadership of Rev. Fred Evans, Pastor of Hayes Chapel Baptist Church of Rose Hill, North Carolina.

At age 18, after being filled with the Holy Spirit, he began his evangelistic training in Fort Walton Beach, Florida under the leadership and training of Pastor Jim Brown, Evangelist Brenda Bynum, and Elder Clarence Oglesby of Sound Christ Gospel Church. Later, the Lord directed Lorenzo to the Beulah Baptist Church of Fort Walton Beach, Florida and the leadership of Pastor Scottie Thigpen where he was ordained. His educational studies include: The Community College of the Air Force, Chapman College, Shaw University School of Divinity, and Freedom Life Bible College. Archbishop Peterson received his Masters in Theological Studies in 2008 and his Doctorate in Theological Studies in 2013 from the Regency Christian College of Jacksonville, Florida.

While serving in the Air Force, he was sent to the state of Alaska where he became the Assistant Pastor to the Rev. Ulysses S. Reid at the Eielson Air Force Base Chapel. Called by God, his next ministry assignment was to pastor at the North Post Chapel in Fairbanks, Alaska. The Lord then sent him to Tacoma, Washington.

Under the direction of Superintendent James T. Watson Sr. of Greater Joy Church of God in Christ, he served as an Assistant to Superintendent Watson, where he was ordained as an Elder.

After relocating to North Carolina in 1988, he began serving as the Youth Pastor of Mt. Zion Baptist Church in Cary, NC. In 1990, he became the pastor of the South Main Street Baptist Church of Louisburg, North Carolina. Upon completion of this assignment, he joined the Church of God in Christ under the leadership of Bishop Leroy Jackson Woolard, Presiding Prelate of the Greater North Carolina Jurisdiction Church of God in Christ and under the tutelage of Superintendent Patrick L. Wooden. On May 19, 2009, he was consecrated by the International Alliance of Bishops as Bishop Primate (Presiding Bishop) where Bishop D. Myles Golphin served as the Chief Consecrator. On July 26, 2018, Archbishop Lorenzo Peterson was enthroned into the Archiepiscopacy as an Archbishop.

Dr. Peterson is a committed member to the Global Conference of Bishops of Raleigh, NC. He is also a member of the Joint College of African American Pentecostal Bishops in Cleveland, Ohio. Archbishop Peterson is a recording artist and author of the book "Pathways to

Perfection" and a workbook entitled "Chosen" designed specifically for clergy, ministers, and church leaders. As an active humanitarian, he serves as the Founder & President of the Help Make a Difference Foundation, Incorporated, a nonprofit organization dedicated to providing youth and adults with vocational, community, and educational support. Archbishop Peterson also serves as a Spiritual Advisor to Asia.

Due to his strong desire to equip and teach God's people, Archbishop Peterson originated the Freedom Life Bible College Incorporated. He also established the International Ministers Covenant Fellowship, Incorporated (IMCF), an organization that equips men and women to fulfill their call in ministry and the International Apostolic Communion (IAC), an organization that provides support and training to various organizations to provide church consultation, pastoral training and mentorship as well as Theological training to all Prelates, Apostles, Overseers, Moderators and Pastors, and Episcopal training.

Archbishop Peterson is a solid prophetic voice in the church and an international conduit in ministry, spreading the Gospel to nations. Dr. Peterson's source of courage and strength is an Old Testament scripture found in Daniel Chapter 11 Verse 32b, "But the people that do know their God shall be strong and do exploits." This scripture also serves as a constant reminder that with a personal relationship with God and all of the power of the Holy Spirit living within…nothing is impossible.

Bishop Lorenzo N. Peterson

New Life Baptist Church

7838 Pacific Avenue SE

P. O. Box 3730 (mailing)

Lacey, Washington 98509-3730

Telephone: (360) 456-5815

Email: newlife@nlbclacey.net

Web page: www.nlbclacey.com

www.ingramcontent.com/pod-product-compliance
Lightning Source LLC
Chambersburg PA
CBHW052106070526
44584CB00017B/2362